More Special Times With God

by
David and Naomi Shibley

Thomas Nelson Publishers
Nashville • Camden • New York

Published in Nashville, Tennessee, by Thomas Nelson, Inc., and distributed in Canada by Lawson Falle, Ltd., Cambridge, Ontario.

Printed in the United States of America.

Scripture quotations are from the NEW KING JAMES VERSION. Copyright © 1979, 1980, Thomas Nelson, Inc., Publishers.

Illustrated by Florence Davis

Library of Congress Cataloging in Publication Data

Shibley, David.
  More special times with God.

  1. Bible—Biography—Meditations. 2. Family—Prayer-
books and devotions—English. I. Shibley, Naomi.
II. Title.
BS571.S49   1984   249   84-3485
ISBN 0-8407-5353-2

To our parents
who first taught us
these stories

Contents

II. Great Prophets of God

III. Men and Women Who Changed the World

IV. The Followers of Jesus

V. Above All Others

A Word to Parents

More than two years have passed since *Special Times With God* was first released. So much has happened. Our sons have grown, and so have we. We are continuing to learn from your many kind letters and from our own experiences. One thing is certain: making family devotions effective is a fine art. It may never be fully mastered, but it can become precisioned yet diverse, structured yet free-flowing.

Just last week we received a precious letter from an eleven-year-old girl in Canada. She suggested there was a need for devotions for the "in-between kids," those who are past the pre-school or early school level, yet who are not early teens. This book is our attempt to meet that need.

Ongoing experience has shown that our suggestions to parents from the previous book are sound. Along with those suggestions, we offer the following observations.

1. *Today's schedules demand flexibility.* It may be impossible for you to have structured family devotions more than two or three times per week. You should not necessarily consider this a limitation to imparting scriptural truth to your children. We are increasingly convinced that "more is caught than taught." Certainly

there is a place for a more formal, didactic impartation of God's Word. What is most important, however, is the reinforcement of that teaching through everyday living. If the central truth for the week is kept in focus, a myriad of living illustrations crop up in the normal patterns of our lives.

2. *Our children don't just need to know about God, they must know God Himself.* Of course, we affirm that our faith rests upon objective truth. However, objective data will never hold the fascination or the devotion of our children. People of all ages hunger for the reality and presence of God. That is why we are not tied to a certain number of hours each week for family devotions. Our children's lives are more profoundly affected by "one divine moment" of His presence than by hours of stale teaching.

Because of this we have given new emphasis to prayer in our home. It is not trite to say that "the family that prays together stays together." In our day, family prayer is more than a good idea; it is necessary for spiritual survival. We strongly urge you to make the "Let's Pray Together" section a springboard to heart-felt prayer to God.

3. *Bible characters serve as good role models for our children.* We live in a world without heroes. Yet all of us, especially children, need examples by which to pattern our behavior. Behavior is often learned, for better or for worse, from others.

These stories of Bible characters chronicle some of the most thrilling sagas of heroism, strength under fire, and earth-moving faith. They provide excellent patterns of conduct for us today.

It is good to remind our children that these Bible characters were not a collection of "supermen." They were ordinary people, subject to the same fears, frustrations, and failures that we are. Yet they excelled in their faith in God and their pursuit of God. James reminds us, "Elijah was a man with a nature like ours . . ." (James 5:17).

10

The Bible asserts that "there is no partiality with God" (Rom. 2:11). What He did in the lives of those men and women, He will do for us as well.

4. *God's Word, hidden in the heart, is our children's greatest weapon against evil.* We continue to stress the importance of memorizing Scripture. Yet, in keeping with our new emphasis on flexibility, we reaffirm that God's Word must be lived out as well as memorized. As you memorize verses with your children, think and pray together for creative ways to see the truth of those verses become yours by experience.

5. *We must remain Christ-centered in our family relationships.* We are overjoyed that our sons feel an evangelistic responsibility to their friends. Our older son, without any prompting, has shared the gospel with several of his schoolmates. In fact, he even shared Christ with his younger brother and prayed with him to receive Christ!

Sadly, the church too often forgets her primary focus. Paul said, "God forbid that I should glory except in the cross of our Lord Jesus Christ, by whom the world has been crucified to me, and I to the world" (Gal. 6:14). While we recognize the importance of sound doctrine, we are not interested just in transmitting a system of theology to the next generation. We are deeply concerned that we give them Christ crucified and risen.

We must convey to our offspring that our primary allegiance is not to any system but to Jesus Christ. The success of the gospel around the world has produced a worldwide Christian community that is very diverse. What all believers have in common is Jesus as Savior and Lord. Our children will be able to relate well to their other brothers and sisters in Christ if we keep Him central in our lives.

This brings us to our final suggestion.

6. *We should impart a world vision to our children.* All people have

some basic inner needs. One primary need is to relate well to others. This need is met first by our relationship with Christ. Flowing from that central relationship between God and believers, we learn to relate well to each other: first in our physical family, then in His family, the church.

There is a second deep need. That is the need for an overarching purpose in life. We are convinced that many, perhaps most, suicides in young people result from a lack of a sense of purpose for their lives.

What greater purpose for living could we impart to our children than to be part of an international team of world-changers! Christ Himself has left us the challenge, "Go therefore and make disciples of all the nations" (Matt. 28:19). The Holy Spirit has given us the enablement. "But you shall receive power when the Holy Spirit has come upon you . . ." (Acts 1:8).

We are living in the most exciting, most perilous era of history. May God bless you as you prepare your children to meet the challenge of their unparalleled times and opportunities.

David and Naomi Shibley
1984

I.

Young People
of the Bible

Isaac
An Obedient Son

Let's Remember:

"'But My covenant I will establish with Isaac, whom Sarah shall bear to you at this set time next year'" (Genesis 17:21).

Let's Listen:

Abraham and Sarah had wanted a son for many years. God had promised them that He would give them a son. Still they waited and waited.

One day Sarah told Abraham the wonderful news. They were going to have a baby! God had turned their sorrow into laughing, and soon Isaac, the promised son, was born. Isaac was a very special child. As he grew, Isaac's parents loved him very much. In fact, it seemed they loved him more each passing day.

Then one day something strange and frightening

happened. God told Abraham to sacrifice Isaac on an altar. Abraham did not understand. But he had always obeyed God, so he set out to obey this strange new order.

Abraham turned to his servants and said, "The lad and I will go yonder and worship, and we will come back to you" (Genesis 22:5). He had faith to believe that somehow God would bring the promised son, Isaac, back to him.

As the father and son climbed the mountain, Isaac realized what God had said to his father. As a strong young man, Isaac could have resisted his father. Yet he obeyed and allowed Abraham to prepare to sacrifice him.

When God saw Abraham's great faithfulness, He sent His angel to keep Abraham from sacrificing Isaac. At that moment God provided an innocent animal for the sacrifice, just as He would one day provide His Son Jesus to be the Lamb of God to take away the sins of the world.

How grateful Abraham and Isaac were to God for His substitute! Isaac had obeyed his father, even though he did not understand the meaning of his father's actions. Are you an obedient child like Isaac?

God had spared Isaac's life. He chose Isaac and his descendants for a very special privilege. It was through the line of Isaac that Jesus would one day come into the world. Isaac's obedience did not bring him harm. Instead God blessed Isaac, and Isaac's family blessed the world.

Isaac's Example Teaches Us:

(1) Obedience brings rewards (see Ephesians 6:1-3);

(2) God protects those who are obedient to Him (see Genesis 22:12).

Let's Pray Together:

Dear God, help me always to be obedient to You, even when I may not understand why. In Jesus' name, amen.

Jacob
He Wouldn't Take
No for an Answer

Let's Remember:

"And Jacob called the name of the place Peniel: 'For I have seen God face to face, and my life is preserved'" (Genesis 32:30).

Let's Listen:

Jacob was very ambitious, which means he wanted to be the best in everything he did. Many times he would scheme to get his way. God did not like this scheming in Jacob and worked with him to correct this fault.

But Jacob had one thing right. He was determined to have the blessings of God on his life. He wanted these blessings so badly, he even tricked his brother Esau into selling him his birthright. In the old days the oldest son in a family had a "birthright." This meant he would receive special blessings that the other children would not receive. But Jacob wanted these blessings for himself, not for his brother, Esau. He talked Esau into trading this special birthright for a big pot of hot cereal when Esau was very hungry.

Something else happened in Jacob's life to show us how very much he wanted God's blessings. One night an angel visited him. He was so determined that the angel would bless him that they got into a fight! Finally the angel asked Jacob what he wanted. Jacob answered, "I will not let You go unless You bless me!" (Genesis 32:26). Then the angel blessed Jacob by changing his name to Israel, which means "Prince with God."

Like the other people we are reading about, Jacob was not a perfect man. But God blessed Jacob because he understood how important it is to have favor with God. Jacob was so serious about having God's blessings that he tricked and schemed to get these blessings. God disciplined Jacob for this bad habit. He does not want us to trick other people. But God wants you, like Jacob, to be serious about doing your best to please Him.

Jacob's Example Teaches Us:

We should diligently seek God and His blessings on our lives. "But without faith it is impossible to please Him, for he who comes to God must believe that He is, and that He is a rewarder of those who diligently seek Him" (Hebrews 11:6).

Let's Pray Together:

Dear God, help me always to seek You with my whole heart. In Jesus' name, amen.

Joseph
The Little Boy
With Big Dreams

Let's Remember:

"'. . . for God sent me before you to preserve life'" (Genesis 45:5).

Let's Listen:

Joseph was Jacob's eleventh son. He was born when Jacob was very old, and Jacob loved Joseph very much. Jacob made Joseph a special coat of many colors. Because of all his father's favors, Joseph's brothers were jealous of him. They thought of an evil plan to get rid of their brother Joseph. After throwing him into a pit, they sold him to some men traveling to Egypt. What a horrible thing to do! Do you see what awful things can happen if we are jealous?

Another reason Joseph's brothers didn't like him was because he had strange dreams. Joseph dreamed

that one day he would be in charge over his brothers, and that they would depend on him to keep them alive. This made his brothers very angry, and that is why they sold him as a slave to the Egyptians.

What would it be like to be a young boy in a strange land away from your family? Joseph was sad. He knew his father thought he was dead. He was also sad when he thought about his brothers' evil deed of selling him.

But even in such a sad and scary time, Joseph kept his faith in God. He remembered the dreams that God had given him. He held on to God's promise that one day he would rule and help many people.

God put Joseph as a slave in the home of an important man named Potiphar. One day while he was away, Potiphar's wife tried to make Joseph do an evil thing. Joseph ran away from her demands because he did not want to sin. He wanted to live a pure life before God. Then Potiphar's wife lied about Joseph and he was thrown into prison.

Can you imagine how Joseph must have felt? He was in prison because he was falsely accused. He was there because he had done right, not because he had done wrong. Still, Joseph kept a firm trust in God. He believed God would bring his dreams to pass.

Because God had given Joseph a special ability to understand the meaning of dreams, he was later taken out of prison to help the ruler. Pharaoh, the ruler of Egypt, was so amazed with the wisdom God had given Joseph, he put him second-in-command of all Egypt. Now Joseph's dreams were coming to pass, for God had remembered Joseph and made his dreams come true.

The Bible tells the wonderful story of how Joseph's brothers and father were brought down to Egypt to visit him (see Genesis 45). It happened just as Joseph had seen in his dreams many years earlier. He forgave his brothers for their evil actions against him. He said, "What you meant for evil God has turned to good. God sent me before you to preserve life" (see Genesis 45:4–5).

Has God put dreams in your heart? Whatever happens, keep your faith in God strong. Even if it takes years, what God has spoken He will bring to pass.

Joseph's Example Teaches Us:

(1) We should run when we are tempted or told to sin (see Genesis 39:12);

(2) We should live for God, even when we don't understand all that is happening to us (see Genesis 39:20);

(3) God will always do what He has promised (see Genesis 41:39–40).

Dear God, help me to hold on to the dreams that You put in my heart. I know that if I trust You, someday You will make them come true. In Jesus' name, amen.

Joshua
He Saw What God Could Do

Let's Remember:

"'This Book of the Law shall not depart from your mouth, but you shall meditate in it day and night, that you may observe to do according to all that is written in it. For then you will make your way prosperous, and then you will have good success'" (Joshua 1:8).

Let's Listen:

Joshua was brave because he knew God was with him. In fact, God had commanded Joshua to be brave. God told Joshua, "Be strong and of good courage. . . . be strong and very courageous" (Joshua 1:6–7).

God was handing over the leadership of the people of Israel from Moses to Joshua. He knew that Joshua would need to be brave to face all the enemies of the new land where they were going.

God had promised Joshua success in everything he did. But Joshua had to do something for that success. He had to listen to God's Word and obey it.

God's Word for us today is the Bible. Promises God gave to Joshua are also promises He makes to you. If you will meditate (think) about what the Bible says, so that you will obey what it says, you will "'make your way prosperous, and then you will have good success'" (Joshua 1:8).

Moses, who had been leader of the people of Israel before Joshua, had done a good job. He had taken them out of Egypt and brought them through the hard years in the wilderness. But Moses had died, and the people of Israel needed a new leader.

Out of all the men of Israel, why did God choose Joshua to be the leader? Perhaps the answer is that

Joshua had great faith in God's Word. He really believed that God would do what He had said.

Joshua knew that God had promised to bring the children of Israel into the Promised Land. It was a beautiful land that flowed "with milk and honey" (see Numbers 13:27).

But there were also giants in the land! Instead of believing God's promise, the people feared the giants. But Joshua, along with a faithful man named Caleb, knew the Lord would keep His promise no matter what! He said, "Only do not rebel against the LORD, nor fear the people of the land, for they are our bread; their protection has departed from them, and the LORD is with us. Do not fear them" (Numbers 14:9).

Joshua believed God's promises. God honored Joshua's great faith. He will honor your faith, too.

Joshua's Example Teaches Us:

(1) We should believe what God says rather than fearing the things around us (see Numbers 14:1–10);

(2) God honors those who will believe His Word (see Joshua 1:1–5);

(3) God brings success to those who think on and obey His Word (see Joshua 1:8).

Dear God, help me to think about Your Word and obey it. Then I know You will bless what I do. In Jesus' name, amen.

Gideon
What Just One
Person Can Do

Let's Remember:

"But Gideon said to them, 'I will not rule over you, nor shall my son rule over you; the LORD shall rule over you'" (Judges 8:23).

Let's Listen:

In a day of false religions, Gideon stood fearlessly for God and for truth. His heart was sad as he saw his own nation, which had once worshiped the true God, now worshiping the false god, Baal. Not only was Gideon sad, he was angry!

One day as Gideon was working, the Angel of the Lord appeared to him. "The LORD is with you, you

mighty man of valor!" the Angel declared (Judges 6:12). Gideon was being chosen by this heavenly messenger to lead the people of Israel to defeat the armies of the Midianites. Although he humbly tried to decline this assignment, he was excited with this new order from the Lord.

The first thing Gideon did was destroy the false gods of Baal. He knew that only after these idols had been overthrown could God bless His people with victory. Although Gideon was just an ordinary young man, God used him to restore worship of the true God to his nation.

You are living in a time much like Gideon's. Often people would rather do as they please than honor the true and living God. Like Gideon you may feel that you are helpless to do anything about it. But look what God did through just one person who loved God and hated evil: Gideon brought righteousness and true faith back to a whole nation. God may be calling you, right now, to be one young person He will use to return many people to His ways. Will you be brave like Gideon and accept His assignment?

Gideon faced times when he doubted that he could carry out such a big order. He asked God for a special sign of His blessing. Gideon placed a fleece of lamb's wool on the ground. He asked the Lord to make the fleece wet and the ground around it dry. Then, the next day, he asked that the ground be wet and the fleece dry. Both times God answered. Gideon knew God was with him.

Then God commanded Gideon to cut the number of his army back to only three hundred men. Those three hundred would have to battle many thousands in the enemy army of the Midianites. Gideon and his men caught the Midianites off guard when they blew their trumpets and shouted, "The sword of the LORD and of Gideon!" (Judges 7:18,20).

God gave Israel a great victory. Because the army was so small, everyone knew that only the Lord could have done such a great thing.

After this the people of Israel wanted to make Gideon their king. But Gideon was still humble in the sight of the Lord. He had paid a dear price to see God restored to His rightful place before the people. Now he could take no glory for himself. "I will not rule over you," Gideon said, "nor shall my son rule over you; the LORD shall rule over you" (Judges 8:23).

The Bible says that during all the rest of the life of Gideon, Israel enjoyed a time of peace (see Judges 8:28).

You may see many things around you that do not please the Lord. What can you, just one ordinary person, do to change things? Remember Gideon. Just one person can restore faith in God. Just one person can bring peace not only for the present but for many years to come. Give your future to God. Let Him show you just what you are to do through His power.

Gideon's Example Teaches Us:

(1) God chooses humble people for great tasks (see Judges 6:11–16);

(2) Just one person can change an entire nation (see Judges 6:14);

(3) When honor comes, only God should receive the glory (see Judges 8:23).

Let's Pray Together:

Dear God, help me to return many people to You and Your ways. In Jesus' name, amen.

Samuel
The Boy Who
Heard God's Voice

Let's Remember:

"But Samuel ministered before the Lord, even as a child . . ." (1 Samuel 2:18).

Let's Listen:

Samuel's very life was an answer to prayer. His mother, Hannah, had wanted a son with all her heart. She had promised God that if she were given a son, she would give him back to the Lord all the days of his life (see 1 Samuel 1:11). God heard Hannah's prayer, and soon Samuel was born.

Hannah obeyed her promise to the Lord and presented the young boy Samuel to Eli the priest. He went to live with Eli and his sons in the tabernacle at Shiloh.

Even as a young boy Samuel was allowed to take

part in some of the duties of being a minister. Did you know that you do not have to be an adult to serve the Lord? You can begin now; you *should* begin now. Our verse to remember says that "Samuel ministered before the LORD, even as a child." You can do that, too.

One night as Samuel was lying in bed, God began to speak to him. The young boy heard His voice say, "Samuel!" (see 1 Samuel 3:4). At first, Samuel thought it was Eli calling for him. So he ran obediently to Eli and said, "Here I am, for you called me" (1 Samuel 3:5). Eli told Samuel that he had not called him. After this happened three times, Eli understood that it was the Lord who was calling Samuel.

God doesn't talk just to big, important people. He talks to children too. God may be calling you! Are you listening?

God talks to us through the Bible. He is speaking to you as we read our Bible verses. But He can also talk to you when you are lying still in your bed, just as He did with Samuel. God can whisper wonderful things in your heart about how He loves you and how He will use your life. Will you listen for His voice?

Because Samuel honored the Lord while he was a child, God honored Samuel when he became an adult. Samuel became a great judge in Israel and led his nation in a time of peace and happiness. He was also given the privilege of anointing Saul, and later David, as kings over Israel. Samuel led a full and godly life because he listened to the voice of the Lord and obeyed Him.

Samuel's Example Teaches Us:

(1) We should be listening for God to speak to us. Most of the time He speaks to us through the Bible. But He also speaks through people like our parents and our pastor. He also can whisper wonderful things in our hearts.

(2) If we honor the Lord while we are young, He will honor us both now and later in life.

Let's Pray Together:

Dear God, I'm so glad You want to talk to me. Help me always to listen for your voice. In Jesus' name, amen.

David
A Heart of
Praise and Service

Let's Remember:

"I will bless the LORD at all times; His praise shall continually be in my mouth" (Psalm 34:1).

Let's Listen:

For long, happy hours, young David would sit on the hillside and sing songs of praise to God. These were beautiful songs he had written while he tended his father's sheep. They make up many of the Psalms we have in the Bible.

David knew that the highest calling in life is to worship God with a pure heart. So he played melodies on his harp and sang praises like, "Praise the LORD! Praise the LORD, O my soul!/While I live I will praise the LORD;/I will sing praises to my God while I have my being" (Psalm 146:1–2).

God saw David and was pleased with his heart of love for Him. He was also pleased with David's heart of service to his earthly father, Jesse, to his brothers, and to King Saul.

One day Jesse asked David to take food to his older brothers who were fighting a battle against the Philistines. David quickly obeyed. When he got to the scene of the conflict he saw that the Philistine giant Goliath had made the armies of Israel afraid. "Who does Goliath think he is, that he would try to defy the armies of the Lord?" David asked (see 1 Samuel 17:26).

God had already given David great power to kill a bear and a lion. Now God was giving David holy boldness against the giant. Young David himself came against mighty Goliath in the name of the Lord of hosts. Goliath was killed, and the armies of Israel won a great victory. God was rewarding David's heart of praise and service, giving him great honor before the eyes of the whole nation.

It was at this very time that God was looking for a man to replace King Saul as new king of Israel. David's brothers were older, stronger, and more talented than he was. But God was looking for a man who would love and serve Him. David was such a person. The Lord said of him, "I have found David the son of Jesse, a man after My own heart, who will do all

My will" (Acts 13:22). So David was anointed king of Israel.

David was not a perfect man. He committed some very serious sins. But he did have an honest heart before the Lord and confessed his sins. God forgave him and cleansed him of his sins, and offered him the strength to start again.

What a great future God has in store for you! He will use you, too, in joyfully serving the Lord and others:

> He also chose David His servant,
> And took him from the sheepfolds;
> From following the ewes that had young
>   He brought him,
> To shepherd Jacob His people,
> And Israel His inheritance.
> So he shepherded them according to
>   the integrity of his heart,
> And guided them by the skillfulness
>   of his hands (Psalm 78:70–72).

David's Example Teaches Us:

(1) Our hearts should be filled with praise to the Lord (see Psalm 34:1);

(2) We should be quick to serve others (see 1 Samuel 17:20);

(3) We should admit our failures to the Lord (see Psalm 51:1–2).

There may be other children who can run faster, make friends easier, and have higher grades in school than you. But remember, God is not looking to see if you can do things better than anyone else. He is looking to see if your desire in life is to love and please Him. If, like David, you have a heart of praise and service, God will lift you to greatness as well.

Let's Pray Together:

Dear God, fill our hearts with praise to You and with service to You and others. In Jesus' name, amen.

Solomon
The World's
Wisest Man

Let's Remember:

"Thus Solomon finished the house of the LORD and the king's house; and Solomon successfully accomplished all that came into his heart to make in the house of the LORD and in his own house" (2 Chronicles 7:11).

Let's Listen:

Solomon was the world's wisest man. He became king of Israel after the death of his father, David. The Lord had told Solomon He would give him whatever he asked.

What would you have asked for? Young King Solomon asked for wisdom. "Give to Your servant an understanding heart," he prayed, "to judge Your people, that I may discern between good and evil" (1 Kings 3:9).

God was very pleased with Solomon's request. Solomon had asked for wisdom instead of riches, but God gave him both. God told Solomon, "And I have also given you what you have not asked: both riches and honor, so that there shall not be anyone like you among the kings all your days" (1 Kings 3:13).

God blessed Solomon greatly throughout his reign as king of Israel. He granted the nation a time of peace. He also allowed Solomon to build a great temple for Him. David, his father, had wanted to build the temple. But God allowed Solomon to do that.

Sometimes God allows children to accomplish dreams and desires their parents have had. It may be that way with you. Perhaps your mother or father wanted to do something great for God and you are the one who will be able to accomplish it.

Solomon made some bad mistakes. But God allowed him to see his dreams fulfilled. As our verse reminds us, "Thus Solomon finished the house of the LORD and the king's house; and Solomon successfully accomplished all that came into his heart to make in the house of the LORD and in his own house" (2 Chronicles 7:11).

Solomon's Example Teaches Us:

(1) We should ask for wisdom from God. The Bible says, "If any of you lacks wisdom, let him ask of God, who gives to all liberally and without reproach, and it will be given to him" (James 1:5).

(2) We should let God put His plans for our lives in our hearts. Then He will let us accomplish them (see 2 Chronicles 7:11).

Let's Pray Together:

Dear God, give me wisdom to make the right choices, and give me ability to do something great for You. In Jesus' name, amen.

Daniel
Living for God
in Hard Times

Let's Remember:

"But Daniel purposed in his heart that he would not defile himself . . ." (Daniel 1:8).

Let's Listen:

Daniel lived for God in hard times. War had separated him from his family and friends. He lived about seven hundred years before Christ, in a foreign land where people worshiped false gods. Even in such hard times, Daniel promised himself that he would live a life pleasing to God.

God honored Daniel greatly for this. God gave Daniel wisdom, health, a happy heart, and favor with the king. Daniel quickly rose to be one of the most important men in the ancient kingdom of Babylon. He did this because God had given Daniel the ability to tell the king just what his dreams meant.

One day King Darius made a law that for the next thirty days no person could pray to God. Instead, they could only ask favors of the king. Daniel saw this as a plan of evil men to trap him in his worship of the true God. The punishment for praying to God in heaven was to be thrown into a den of hungry lions.

When Daniel heard the king's order not to pray to God, he did not have to question whether or not he would keep on praying. Daniel had *already,* years before, decided he would live for God, no matter what the cost. Likewise, we must determine to live for the Lord before the big tests come.

Because he kept on praying to God, Daniel was thrown into the lions' den. But God did something wonderful! He closed the mouths of the lions. Daniel gladly announced to the king, "My God sent His angel and shut the lions' mouths, so that they have not hurt me, because I was found innocent before Him; and also, O king, I have done no wrong before you" (Daniel 6:22).

This made the king change his mind. He declared the God of Daniel to be the true and living God. He proclaimed,

> For He is the living God,
> And steadfast forever;

His kingdom is the one which shall not
  be destroyed,
And His dominion shall endure to the end.
He delivers and rescues,
And He works signs and wonders
In heaven and on earth,
Who has delivered Daniel from the power of
  the lions (Daniel 6:26–27).

What a great God we serve! He is worthy of our love and obedience, even in hard times.

Daniel's Example Teaches Us:

(1) We should purpose in our hearts to live for God before trials ever come (see Daniel 1:8);

(2) Prayer is so important that some people have been willing to die for the privilege of talking to God (see Daniel 6:16);

(3) God will defend us if we live for Him when nobody else does (see Daniel 6:22).

Let's Pray Together:

Dear God, may our lives always honor You, no matter where we are. In Jesus' name, amen.

Shadrach, Meshach, and Abed-Nego Loyalty to God in the Fire

Let's Remember:

". . . our God whom we serve is able to deliver us from the burning fiery furnace, and He will deliver us" (Daniel 3:17).

Let's Listen:

These three Hebrew boys were friends of Daniel, whom we read about earlier. Along with Daniel, these three teenagers decided to live for God even when it was unpopular and dangerous. Nebuchadnezzar, the king of Babylon, had made a decree that no one could worship any god other than the golden image or idol that he had made.

Shadrach, Meshach, and Abed-Nego knew that this would be a terrible sin against the only true God. They knew in the Ten Commandments that God had said, "You shall have no other gods before Me. You shall not make for yourselves any carved image, or any likeness of anything that is in heaven above, or that is in the earth beneath, or that is in the water under the earth; you shall not bow down to them nor serve them" (Exodus 20:3–5). These Hebrew boys had decided they would obey God's command.

King Nebuchadnezzar warned them that if they disobeyed his decree to worship the golden image, they would be thrown into the fiery furnace. But they said, "O Nebuchadnezzar, we have no need to answer you in this matter" (Daniel 3:16). Their minds were already made up to obey God, long before this test came along! Their loyalty to God was a settled fact. Although they honored their king, they could say with Peter, "We ought to obey God rather than men" (Acts 5:29).

Do you know what loyalty means? Loyalty means to be faithful no matter what happens. Shadrach, Meshach, and Abed-Nego had decided to stay faithful to God even if they were burnt up in the fiery furnace.

But God blessed their loyalty and confidence in Him. A mighty fourth Man came into the fiery furnace with these three boys. Nebuchadnezzar said this fourth Man looked like the Son of God (see Daniel 3:25). As He was with these young men, Jesus will be with you in your fiery tests, too.

God kept Shadrach, Meshach, and Abed-Nego

even from being burned by the fire. When the king saw what mighty things the living God could do, he released Shadrach, Meshach, and Abed-Nego, and promoted them in his kingdom.

You may face some heated tests in your life. But if you decide now to stay faithful to God no matter what happens, He will protect you too.

Shadrach, Meshach, and Abed-Nego's Example Teaches Us:

(1) We should decide to be faithful to the Lord before the fiery tests come;

(2) We must never bend to pressure not to serve the living God;

(3) We must obey God rather than men, if men tell us to disobey God (see Acts 5:29);

(4) God will honor our loyalty to Him (see Daniel 3:30).

Let's Pray Together:

Dear God, right now I choose to be faithful to You when the heated tests of life come. When I need special courage, I know You will be with me. In Jesus' name, amen.

Timothy
Learning from Others

Let's Remember:

"And that from childhood you have known the Holy Scriptures, which are able to make you wise for salvation through faith which is in Christ Jesus" (2 Timothy 3:15).

Let's Listen:

Timothy was a very fortunate boy. Both his mother and grandmother had taught him the ways of the Lord. He had been taught God's Word since he was a child. So Timothy first learned about God and His ways from the Bible and from his godly mother and grandmother.

Someone loves you like that, too. Someone is reading this book with you right now. That person wants you to know the Holy Scriptures, too. Just as Timothy's mother and grandmother taught him, the per-

47

son reading this book with you is teaching you God's ways.

Timothy also had a very special friend. This friend was the apostle Paul. Paul knew that God's hand was on Timothy in a special way. He knew God had chosen Timothy to be a preacher of the good news about Jesus. Paul loved Timothy as if he were his own son.

Because of Paul's love for Timothy, he took Timothy on trips with him. In this way Timothy was able to watch the great apostle as he preached and prayed for the people. No doubt Timothy learned much about how to preach and care for people by watching how the apostle Paul lived.

Soon young Timothy had a church of his own where he was pastor. Paul continued to keep in touch with Timothy by writing him letters of instruction on how to build the church. These letters are in the Bible today as the books of First and Second Timothy. Paul encouraged Timothy to work with other men just as he had worked with him. "And the things that you have heard from me among many witnesses, commit these to faithful men who will be able to teach others also" (2 Timothy 2:2).

Because Timothy was young, some people did not think he would make a good pastor. But Paul told

Timothy, "Let no one despise your youth, but be an example to the believers in word, in conduct, in love, in spirit, in faith, in purity" (1 Timothy 4:12). God is telling you that too. Right now, while you are young, you can be an example to others by the way you live.

Timothy's Example Teaches Us:

(1) It is important to know the Bible. God's Word can make us wise for salvation through faith in Christ (see 2 Timothy 3:15);

(2) We should learn from godly parents and grand-parents (see 2 Timothy 1:5);

(3) We should learn from our pastor and other godly people God brings into our lives (see 2 Timothy 2:2).

Let's Pray Together:

Dear God, even while I'm young, help me to be an example to others by the way I live. In Jesus' name, amen.

II.

Great Prophets of God

Elijah
Fire from Heaven

Let's Remember:

"'Hear me, O LORD, hear me, that this people may know that You are the LORD God, and that You have turned their hearts back to You again'" (1 Kings 18:37).

Let's Listen:

Elijah was one of the greatest prophets in the history of Israel. A prophet is a person used by God as His messenger to warn others.

Elijah was fearless in standing for God and for what was right. He challenged the false god Baal and its worshipers on Mount Carmel. He restored a young boy to life by God's power. He called evil King Ahab and Queen Jezebel to account for their evil deeds.

God blessed Elijah for his boldness in preaching truth. Like Enoch, God let Elijah go to heaven without dying. He was taken up into heaven by a whirlwind in a chariot of fire (see 2 Kings 2:11).

One of the greatest stories from Elijah's life is the story of how God brought fire from heaven on Mount Carmel. Elijah had declared that because of Israel's worship of false gods there would be a long time with no rain. Still many people in Israel persisted in worshiping the false god of Baal.

Elijah challenged the people to make up their minds who they would worship and serve. "How long will you falter between two opinions?" he asked. "If the LORD is God, follow Him; but if Baal, then follow him" (1 Kings 18:21). Still the people were undecided.

So Elijah had the worshipers of Baal ask their false god to answer by fire when they prayed to him. All day long they cried and cried to the false god. They even cut themselves to try to show Baal they were serious. But no answer.

Elijah sat by and heckled them. He said, "Maybe Baal is busy, or maybe he's gone on a trip. Maybe he's just asleep and needs to be awakened!" (see 1 Kings 18:27). Elijah knew that it was foolish to pray to a god of stone or brass. He knew that only the true and living God can hear and answer prayer.

Finally Elijah built an altar to the true God, the Father of our Lord Jesus Christ. The worshipers of Baal looked on, tired from their crying out to nobody. Elijah said, "Now drench my altar with water." Three times they poured water on the altar until water flowed into the trench around the altar.

Then Elijah prayed a simple prayer:

"LORD God of Abraham, Isaac, and Israel, let it be known this day that you are God in Israel, and that I am Your servant, and that I have done all these things at your word. Hear me, O LORD, hear me, that this people may know that You are the LORD God, and that You have turned their hearts back to You again" (1 Kings 18:36–37).

Right away, fire came down from heaven! It consumed the sacrifice, the altar, and even the water around the altar! The people were no longer undecided. They began to shout, "The LORD, He is God! The LORD, He is God!" (1 Kings 18:39).

The worshipers of Baal were destroyed. The people's hearts were turned again to the Lord, and God brought an end to the lack of rain. The land had blessing again. Why? Because fearless Elijah had called the people back to God.

Elijah's Example Teaches Us:

(1) It is important to worship and serve the true God and Him alone;

(2) We should never be afraid to stand for what is right.

Let's Pray Together:

Dear God, help me always to stand for truth so that the hearts of people will be turned to You. In Jesus' name, amen.

Elisha
Twice the Power
of His Teacher

Let's Remember:

"And so it was, when they had crossed over, that Elijah said to Elisha, 'Ask! What may I do for you, before I am taken away from you?' And Elisha said, 'Please let a double portion of your spirit be upon me'" (2 Kings 2:9).

Let's Listen:

Elisha was much like Timothy because he had a special older friend. Just as Timothy was taught by Paul, so Elisha was taught by the prophet Elijah.

Elisha came from a wealthy family. One day as he was plowing one of his father's fields, Elijah found him and placed his mantle on young Elisha. A mantle was worn like a coat. When it was given away by the owner, it was a sign that the calling and power of his life were being given to the person who received the mantle. This meant that God had chosen Elisha to take Elijah's place one day.

Elisha ran home and told his parents. They celebrated by having a big feast. Then, Elisha left home to go with Elijah. Everyone knew it was a very big honor to be chosen by God to be a prophet.

As Elisha traveled with the older prophet, he watched how God used Elijah in wonderful ways. Elisha longed to be powerfully used by God as well. When the time came for Elijah to be taken up into heaven, he asked young Elisha what he might do for him before he went away. Elisha answered, "Please let a double portion of your spirit be upon me" (2 Kings 2:9). Elisha knew God's power had rested on Elijah for many years. Now he wanted that same power doubled so he, too, could speak out for God.

Elijah answered, "You have asked a hard thing. Nevertheless, if you see me when I am taken from you, it shall be so for you; but if not, it shall not be so" (2 Kings 2:10).

So Elisha stayed very close to Elijah. Then, on the day when Elijah was taken up to heaven, Elisha was there to see it. His request was granted.

Right away, people knew God's power was now on Elisha. He began to do miracles. In fact, Elisha performed fourteen miracles in his lifetime. Elijah had performed seven. Do you see? Elisha received twice the power of his teacher, just as he had requested.

Elisha had trained in secret under Elijah. Now he was brought to greatness. By the way, are you letting a godly older person, someone like your pastor or parents, teach you?

Elisha's Example Teaches Us:

(1) We can learn from the experiences of others;

(2) We can trust God to use us in even greater ways for the challenging days ahead.

Let's Pray Together:

Dear God, help me to learn from those who are older and wiser than I am. In Jesus' name, amen.

Isaiah
He Saw the Coming King

Let's Remember:

For unto us a Child is born,
Unto us a Son is given;
And the government will be upon His shoulder.
And His name will be called
Wonderful, Counselor, Mighty God,
Everlasting Father, Prince of Peace (Isaiah 9:6).

Let's Listen:

Isaiah was a prophet to the nation of Judah. After the good King Uzziah died, God revealed His holiness to Isaiah.

When Isaiah saw how just and holy God is, he knew he was not prepared for his important job. Isaiah confessed his sins, and God forgave him and promised to use him. "Also I heard the voice of the Lord, saying: 'Whom shall I send,/And who will go for Us?' Then I said, 'Here am I! Send me'" (Isaiah 6:8).

God revealed to Isaiah many wonderful things that would one day happen. Most wonderful of all was God's promise to send His Son to bring us salvation and forgiveness. The One that God would send would one day rule the world in righteousness.

Of the increase of His government and peace
There will be no end,
Upon the Throne of David and over His kingdom,
To order and establish it with judgment and justice
From that time forward, even forever.
The zeal of the LORD of hosts will perform this
(Isaiah 9:7).

God spoke further of this Savior He would send:

Surely He has borne our griefs
And carried our sorrows;
Yet we esteemed Him stricken,
Smitten by God, and afflicted.
But He was wounded for our transgressions,
He was bruised for our iniquities;
The chastisement for our peace was upon Him,
And by His stripes we are healed (Isaiah 53:4–5).

We know that God was talking about Jesus, His wonderful Son, whom He would send into the world. But just think! Isaiah got a picture of this coming Savior hundreds of years before He was born.

Isaiah's Example Teaches Us:
We can rest assured that God has a plan for His world. Even when things looked very dark, God promised Isaiah that a better time was coming and that He would rule in righteousness.

Let's Pray Together:
Thank you, God, that I know Jesus will rule one day over the whole world. I'm glad that my future is in Your loving hands. In Jesus' name, amen.

Jeremiah
Joy in The
Midst of Sadness

Let's Remember:
"'But let him who glories glory in this,/That he understands and knows Me,/That I am the LORD exercising lovingkindness, judgment, and righteousness

in the earth./For in these I delight,' says the LORD"
(Jeremiah 9:24).

Let's Listen:

Jeremiah did not have a very happy life. In fact, he
is often called "the weeping prophet."

When he saw the sins of the people and knew that
they would not turn from them, he knew that God
would then judge the people. This is what happened,
and it made Jeremiah cry. How he longed to see the
people live for the Lord! But they would not listen to
him.

Jeremiah did not have many friends. When he told
the people that God would judge their sins, the people turned against him. Sometimes Jeremiah was
thrown into jail for telling the truth. One time he was
thrown into a muddy pit and left to die. But God res-
cued him.

Jeremiah worked for many years to write down
God's Word. When Baruch, Jeremiah's servant, began
to read God's message to the king, the king became
angry. He tore up the scroll on which it was written
and threw it in the fire. Imagine! Twenty years of
work going up in smoke!

Still, Jeremiah would not be discouraged. He wrote
it all over again along with other messages God gave
to him. Because Jeremiah was faithful, God allowed

him to write two books of the Bible: the book of Jeremiah and the book of Lamentations. He also may have written some of the Psalms.

Even in such terrible times, Jeremiah learned to find joy in walking with the Lord. He loved God's Word very much. "Your words were found," Jeremiah said to the Lord, "and I ate them,/And Your word was to me the joy and rejoicing of my heart" (Jeremiah 15:16). Jeremiah was saying that God's Word was food for his inner life, his soul.

Also, in those dark days Jeremiah learned the value of prayer. God gave Jeremiah a wonderful promise. It is a promise for us as well. "Call to Me, and I will answer you, and show you great and mighty things, which you do not know" (Jeremiah 33:3).

In the hard times of life, Jeremiah had found the secret of having joy. What was it? Jeremiah walked with the Lord.

Jeremiah's Example Teaches Us:

In life's hard times we can have joy inside by walking with the Lord.

Let's Pray Together:

Thank You, God, that I can have a happy heart wherever I go because You are with me. In Jesus' name, amen.

Ezekiel
A Special Kind of Person

Let's Remember:

"'I will give you a new heart and put a new spirit within you; I will take the heart of stone out of your flesh and give you a heart of flesh'" (Ezekiel 36:26).

Let's Listen:

Ezekiel, like many of the Old Testament prophets, also lived in unhappy times. For much of his life he was forced to live in the pagan city of Babylon. He told his fellow Jewish people that they were in this strange land because of their sins. Some believed what Ezekiel was saying, but many did not.

Still, Ezekiel preached the Word of the Lord. He taught that God does not delight in punishing people. Instead, God wants people to turn from their evil ways. God spoke to Ezekiel and said, "Say to them: 'As I live,' says the Lord GOD, 'I have no pleasure in the death of the wicked, but that the wicked turn from his way and live. Turn, turn from your evil ways! For why should you die, O house of Israel?'" (Ezekiel 33:11).

God also told Ezekiel that He was looking for a prophet who would pray that He would forgive and cleanse the people. "So I sought for a man," God said, "who would make a wall, and stand in the gap before Me on behalf of the land, that I should not destroy it . . ." (Ezekiel 22:30).

But here's the sad part. God said, "I found no one."

We also live in an evil time. God is still looking for special people, Christians who will "stand in the gap" and pray for others. Will you be that special kind of person?

In our memory verse God said, "I will put a new heart in you!" When we receive Jesus, we receive a "new heart." That means we really want to love and serve the Lord and to pray for other people.

Ezekiel's Example Teaches Us:

(1) God does not want the wicked to die without Him. Instead He wants them to repent (see Ezekiel 33:11);

(2) God is looking for a special kind of person who will pray to Him in behalf of others (see Ezekiel 22:30);

(3) When we come to Jesus, we receive a new heart of love for God (see Ezekiel 36:26).

Let's Pray Together:
Dear God, help me to be that special kind of person who will pray for others. In Jesus' name, amen.

Hosea
God's Great Mercy

Let's Remember:
"Sow for yourselves righteousness;/Reap in mercy;/ Break up your fallow ground,/For it is time to seek the LORD,/Till He comes and rains righteousness on you" (Hosea 10:12).

Let's Listen:
Hosea was broken-hearted. He saw that God's people were sinning and disobeying the Lord. They were doing many things that angered God.

Over and over, Hosea told the people that God still loved them, even though they were sinning against

Him. God told Hosea to do some hard things to get the people's attention. Hosea told the people that God must judge sin. But he also told the people how very much God loved them and desired to forgive them.

Hosea reminded the people that there is always a payment for sinning. He told them that God had said, "They sow the wind, and reap the whirlwind" (Hosea 8:7). God was very angry because of the sin of the people. Yet, in the midst of His holy anger, He showed His amazing love and mercy. "I will not execute the fierceness of My anger," God said, ". . . For I am God, and not man,/The Holy One in your midst;/ And I will not come with terror" (Hosea 11:9).

How very much Hosea wanted the people to turn back to the Lord! He knew that when they did, God would forgive them and bless them. That's why Hosea said,

> Sow for yourselves righteousness;
> Reap in mercy;
> Break up your fallow ground,
> For it is time to seek the LORD,
> Till He comes and rains righteousness
>   on you (Hosea 10:12).

Hosea's Example Teaches Us:

(1) Even when we turn away from God, He does not turn His love away from us (see Hosea 11:9);

(2) God wants to bless His people with righteousness (see Hosea 10:12).

Let's Pray Together:

Thank You, God, that Your love for me never stops, even when I may fail You and others. In Jesus' name, amen.

Joel
God Is the
Great Restorer

Let's Remember:

"And it shall come to pass/That whoever calls on the name of the LORD/Shall be saved" (Joel 2:32).

Let's Listen:

God told Joel thrilling things about the future. Then, Joel told the people what God had told him.

For one thing, God told Joel that there was a great

day of judgment coming for the whole world. But God also promised a wonderful time when He would restore to those who obeyed Him all that the devil had taken away. Many people felt they had wasted years of their lives. In His loving power, God promised, "I will restore to you the years . . ." (Joel 2:25).

Through Joel, God spoke further of this wonderful period of time.

". . . I will pour out My Spirit on all flesh;
Your sons and your daughters shall prophesy,
Your old men shall dream dreams,
Your young men shall see visions;
And also on My menservants and on My
 maidservants
I will pour out My Spirit in those days" (Joel 2:28–29).

He told us the Holy Spirit would be given to His new people, the church.

These days in which we live are a wonderful time of spiritual harvest when many people are coming to Jesus. In this time, God saves everyone who asks for His salvation. "And it shall come to pass/That whoever calls on the name of the LORD/Shall be saved" (Joel 2:32).

71

Joel's Example Teaches Us:

(1) God will restore what the devil has taken away (see Joel 2:25);

(2) Whoever asks God to save him, calling on the name of Jesus, will be saved (see Joel 2:32).

Let's Pray Together:

Thank you, God, that Your salvation and Your Spirit are being poured out all over the world. In Jesus' name, amen.

Amos
God's Anger at Sin

Let's Remember:

"'But let justice run down like water, And righteousness like a mighty stream'" (Amos 5:24).

Let's Listen:

The book of Amos tells us how serious God is about sin. Amos was angry at evil. The very people who claimed to know God hurt and mistreated each other. They paid no attention to God's holy law.

The people had fooled themselves. They believed if

they did religious things, it didn't matter how they lived. Amos told them God did not simply want feasts or holidays in His honor. Instead, God wanted people who would show mercy and justice to each other. "'But let justice run down like water, And righteousness like a mighty stream'" (Amos 5:24).

Amos taught the people that God would not go with them unless they turned from their sins. The people were going one way, God was going another. "Can two walk together, unless they are agreed?" God asked (Amos 3:3).

Amos's anger is a mirror of God's anger against sin. His holiness cannot look on sin. That is why Amos urged the people, "Seek good and not evil,/That you may live;/So the LORD God of hosts will be with you . . ." (Amos 5:14).

When people do not obey God's word, God may remove His word from those people. This would be a very dangerous thing. How could we possibly live without God's word? That is why God warns us to hear His word and obey it.

> "Behold, the days are coming," says the Lord GOD,
> "That I will send a famine on the land,
> Not a famine of bread,
> Nor a thirst for water,
> But of hearing the words of the LORD" (Amos 8:11).

But we also see God's great mercy! He promises a time when His people will return to Him. Then God will restore His people to their land. "'I will plant them in their land,/And no longer shall they be pulled up/From the land I have given them,'/Says the LORD your God" (Amos 9:15).

Amos's Example Teaches Us:
God is more interested in how we act than in our being "religious."

Let's Pray Together:
Dear God, help me to live a just and honest life from my heart. I know that is pleasing to You. In Jesus' name, amen.

Obadiah
A Warning against Pride

Let's Remember:
"'The pride of your heart has deceived you'" (Obadiah 1:3).

Let's Listen:

Obadiah was a prophet who wrote a short book with an important message. The message is to watch out for pride.

Pride is thinking more of yourself than you ought to think. The Bible warns against that. "For I say, through the grace given to me, to everyone who is among you, not to think of himself more highly than he ought to think, but to think soberly . . ." (Romans 12:3). That means we are to thank God honestly for what He has given us, and never think *we* should get the glory instead of Him.

This warning against pride runs all through the Bible. Instead of showing pride, we are to humble ourselves and bow down before the Lord. "Humble yourselves in the sight of the Lord, and He will lift you up" (James 4:10).

Not much is known about the prophet Obadiah. He did God's will and bowed down before Him. His name means "servant" or "worshiper of God." These two things are what pride is *not*.

Instead of being proud, we should be servants to the Lord and to others.

Obadiah's Example Teaches Us:

(1) We must resist the temptation to be proud:

"Pride goes before destruction,/And a haughty spirit before a fall" (Proverbs 16:18);

(2) God wants us to worship Him always.

Let's Pray Together:

Dear God, keep my heart from pride. Make me humble before You. In Jesus' name, amen.

Jonah
Going God's Way

Let's Remember:

"Jonah arose and went to Nineveh, according to the word of the Lord" (Jonah 3:2).

Let's Listen:

Children everywhere love the Bible story of how Jonah was swallowed by the great fish. The best way to hear this story is to have the person who is reading this book with you read the first three chapters of the book of Jonah to you.

Do you remember what happened? God had told Jonah to go to Nineveh and tell the people of that great city to turn from their sins. If they did not, God said He would destroy the city.

But Jonah didn't like the people of Nineveh. He *wanted* God to judge them. So he did not go to warn them, as God had told him. Many times we are like that, aren't we? We want to punish people. God wants to forgive them.

Jonah went on a boat away from the city of Nineveh. He was not obeying what God told him to do. So God allowed a great storm to come. Jonah confessed to the sailors that he caused the storm by going against God's command. Even though they didn't want to, the men had to throw him overboard.

God had prepared a great fish to swallow Jonah. Gulp! There he was, tucked away inside the stomach of the great fish. Jonah stayed in that fish for three days and nights. Don't you imagine he thought many times, "If only I had gone to Nineveh as God told me!"?

God delivered Jonah from the fish in an awful, yet amazing way. The Bible says that after Jonah prayed and asked God to deliver him, the fish vomited him onto dry ground (see Jonah 2:10).

Now, Jonah was ready to obey God. You and I would be, too! He went quickly to Nineveh and told the people they must repent of their sins. Nineveh did

repent and God spared that great city from His judgment.

You can be sure Jonah always obeyed the Lord after that! Jonah learned that it's always better to go God's way.

Jonah's Example Teaches Us:

(1) If we do not obey what God says, we may be in very big trouble;

(2) The Lord will use us to do His will when we decide to obey Him.

Let's Pray Together:

Dear God, help me always to obey You right away when You speak to me. In Jesus' name, amen.

Micah
What God Wants from You

Let's Remember:

He has shown you, O man, what is good;
And what does the Lord require of you

But to do justly,
To love mercy,
And to walk humbly with your God? (Micah 6:8).

Let's Listen:

God told Micah what He wanted from His people. First, God told His people that He wanted them to "do justly." That means we are to be fair and do the things that are right. When you're playing with the other kids in your neighborhood, are you fair? Or do you cheat? God calls on us to do the right thing.

Next, God said we are to "love mercy." When your brothers or sisters are in trouble, do you like to see them punished? Do you think, "Boy, I sure hope they get it. After all, they deserve it!"

But wait a minute. Stop and think about what we all deserve. Because of our sins we all deserve punishment. But God has mercy on us when we come to Him. Now God is asking us to do the same.

Finally, God said we are to "walk humbly" with Him. Do you see? We are back to the point of pride. God is saying, "Don't get the big head. Walk with Me with a thankful heart. Then I can bless you."

Micah's Example Teaches Us:

(1) We are to be fair and do what is right;

(2) We are not only to show mercy, we are to *love* to show mercy;

(3) We are to walk humbly before God.

Let's Pray Together:

Dear God, help me to do what is right, to be merciful to others, and to walk humbly before You. In Jesus' name, amen.

Nahum
God's Great Power

Let's Remember:

"The LORD is good,/A stronghold in the day of trouble;/And He knows those who trust in Him" (Nahum 1:7).

Let's Listen:

Do you remember the city of Nineveh? The city had repented at the preaching of Jonah. Now it was many years later. Nineveh had gone back into its sin. And now God had to bring judgment.

Nahum was the prophet who told the people of

Nineveh that God must now bring judgment to them because of their sin. But Nahum also had some good news. The Lord is a stronghold for those who trust in Him. That means that even in a time of judgment, God protects those who turn away from their sins.

There is much sin in our world today. At some time, though we don't know just when, God must judge the world's sin. This will happen when Jesus comes again, to judge the living and the dead. And when that time comes, you do not need to be afraid if you trust the Lord and do His will. Remember, "The LORD is good,/ A stronghold in the day of trouble;/And He knows those who trust in Him" (Nahum 1:7).

Nahum's Example Teaches Us:

God will protect those who trust in Him, even in times of trouble.

Let's Pray Together:

Thank You, God, that You will protect me in times of trouble because I trust in You. In Jesus' name, amen.

Habakkuk
Living by Faith

Let's Remember:
"'. . . But the just shall live by his faith'" (Habakkuk 2:4).

Let's Listen:
Habakkuk wanted to see God's holiness present in his nation. As he looked around he saw the people turning from God's ways and paying no attention to His holy law. This caused Habakkuk to cry to God.

He asked God why His will was not being done among His people. He reminded God as he prayed, "You are of purer eyes than to behold evil, and cannot look on wickedness" (Habakkuk 1:13).

God encouraged Habakkuk to live by faith. The Lord gave Habakkuk a picture of what He would do. God let the prophet look into the future and see that one day the people would remember God's holiness and walk in His ways.

He told Habakkuk,

> "Write the vision
> And make it plain on tablets,
> That he may run who reads it.
> For the vision is yet for an appointed time;
> But at the end it will speak, and it will not lie.
> Though it tarries, wait for it;
> Because it will surely come,
> It will not tarry" (Habakkuk 2:2–3).

God was telling Habakkuk to have faith in His promises. Faith is trusting God. Faith is counting on what God has said. Habakkuk did this. That is why the Bible calls him a "just" man. A just person is someone God sees as good. We become good in God's sight by our faith in Him.

Habakkuk saw a future which was very bright. "For the earth will be filled/With the knowledge of the glory of the LORD,/As the waters cover the sea" (Habakkuk 2:14).

Habakkuk may not have lived to see all of God's promises come to pass. But he held firm to those promises. Even when his faith was tested, Habakkuk declared, "The LORD God is my strength;/He will make my feet like deer's feet,/And He will make me walk on my high hills" (Habakkuk 3:19).

Habakkuk's Example Teaches Us:

(1) We should live by faith in what God says (see Habakkuk 2:4);

(2) We should pray that other people will know God is holy (see Habakkuk 1);

(3) We should trust God even when we don't see answers right away (see Habakkuk 2:2–3).

Let's Pray Together:

Dear God, help me always to put my trust in You and in what You say. In Jesus' name, amen.

Zephaniah
Turning While
There Is Time

Let's Remember:

"The LORD your God in your midst,
The Mighty One, will save;

He will rejoice over you with gladness,
He will quiet you in His love,
He will rejoice over you with singing"
　　(Zephaniah 3:17).

Let's Listen:

Zephaniah had a big job. He had to warn the people who were sinning against God that there was a great day of judgment coming. When the Bible talks about "judgment," it means that God will one day make everyone pay for his or her sins. Zephaniah warned the people that the judgment day was not far off. "The great day of the LORD is near;/It is near and hastens quickly" (Zephaniah 1:14).

He warned the people to turn to God before the judgment came. The Bible teaches that there is a payment for sinning. "For the wages of sin is death . . ." (Romans 6:23).

But that's not all! Jesus has paid for our sins on the cross. He took the judgment for sin on Himself. When we trust Him and accept His payment for our sins, we will not come into judgment for them.

Yes, God must judge sin. But He also wants to forgive us of our sins: "For the wages of sin is death, but the gift of God is eternal life in Christ Jesus our Lord" (Romans 6:23).

God spoke a word of hope to the people through Zephaniah. They would not keep sinning against the Lord. God would draw them back to Himself. God, the Mighty One, would save them. God promised His people, ". . . I will bring you back, . . ./For I will give you fame and praise/Among all the people of the earth . . ." (Zephaniah 3:20).

Zephaniah's Example Teaches Us:
(1) We must warn people that God will judge sin (see Zephaniah 1:14);

(2) We must offer hope in God's forgiveness to those who turn from their sins (see Zephaniah 2:1–3).

Let's Pray Together:
Dear God, may those who are living away from You turn to You so their sins may be forgiven. In Jesus' name, amen.

Haggai
Building Again

Let's Remember:
" 'The silver is Mine, and the gold is Mine,' says the LORD of hosts" (Haggai 2:8).

Let's Listen:
God gave Haggai a very special job. For many years the temple where the people had worshiped God was in ruins. God told Haggai to encourage the people to rebuild the temple so they would be serious again about worshiping God.

The people were poor. Though they earned money, they never seemed to have enough. There are many people like that today.

God told Haggai there was a reason why the people were poor. It was because they had been more concerned about building their own houses than building the house of God. While the temple of God was in ruins, God's people were living in nice houses. God said they should be concerned about His house first.

Today, the temple of God is the church, not a building made with hands, but the whole family of God. We should put our brothers and sisters in Christ first because the church is where God's Spirit lives.

The important lesson to learn from the prophet Haggai is that God wants His people to be more concerned about His house as a place of love and worship than they are about their own houses.

Are you paying as much attention to the things that are important to God as you are to the things that are important to you?

When we are paying attention to the things God says are important, God promises to supply all our needs. After all, all the wealth of the world belongs to God. "'The silver is Mine, and the gold is Mine,' says the LORD of hosts" (Haggai 2:8).

Haggai's Example Teaches Us:

(1) We should remember that all wealth belongs to God (see Haggai 2:8);

(2) We should pay attention to the things God says are important (see Haggai 2:7–8).

Dear God, help me to pay attention to those things that are important to You. In Jesus' name, amen.

Zechariah
A World Where
the Lord Is King

Let's Remember:

"'Not by might nor by power, but by My Spirit,'/Says the LORD of hosts" (Zechariah 4:6).

Let's Listen:

Zechariah was born in a foreign country, away from his homeland. Like Haggai, he wanted to see his people love and serve God. But many times, the people ignored Zechariah's preaching. Still he continued to call to them and to give them God's message: "'Return to Me,' says the LORD of hosts, 'and I will return to you,' says the LORD of hosts" (Zechariah 1:3).

The prophet encouraged the people by telling them how much God loved them. Even though they

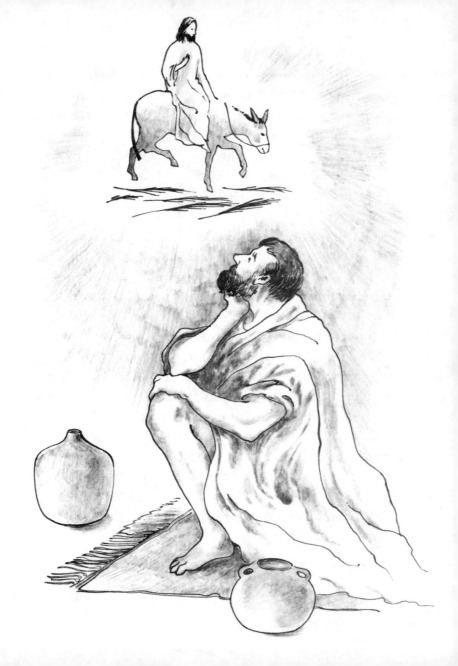

sinned against God, they were still "the apple of His eye" (Zechariah 2:8). God would one day bring His people into true freedom. They would again know the joy of living for God. How would this happen? God answered, "'Not by might nor by power, but by My Spirit,' says the LORD of hosts" (Zechariah 4:6).

God let Zechariah see into the future. He saw a world where the Lord would be King over all nations. God let him have perhaps the clearest picture of any Old Testament prophet of the coming Messiah. The prophet foretold, "Behold your King is coming to you;/He is just and having salvation,/Lowly and riding on a donkey" (Zechariah 9:9). Jesus rode on a donkey the day He entered Jerusalem!

Yes, Zechariah saw that one day the Lord would be King over all the earth. "And the LORD shall be King over all the earth./In that day it shall be—/'The LORD is one,'/And His name one" (Zechariah 14:9).

Zechariah's Example Teaches Us:

(1) God turns to us when we turn to Him (see Zechariah 1:3);

(2) We should remember that one day the Lord will reign over all the earth (see Zechariah 14:9).

Dear God, help me to live for You by letting Your
Spirit work in me. In Jesus' name, amen.

Malachi
God Loves Families

Let's Remember:

"'But to you who fear My name/The Sun of Righteousness shall arise/With healing in His wings . . .'"
(Malachi 4:2).

Let's Listen:

God loves families very much. That is why He told
His prophet Malachi to warn the people against sepa-
rating from their families. Moms, Dads, and children
are to stay united to each other. You see, God knows
that the best way for people to love Him is in happy,
healthy families. The Bible says, "God sets the solitary
in families . . ." (Psalm 68:6).

God told husbands to take good care of their wives
and to love them. He said, ". . . Take heed to your

spirit,/And let none deal treacherously with the wife of his youth" (Malachi 2:15).

God was teaching the people about what makes families happy. First, God said that families are to keep their promises to each other (see Malachi 2:14–16). Then, God said that we are to be good stewards of the money He gives us (see Malachi 3:8–10). A steward is someone who keeps something that is owned by another person. The money we have isn't really ours. It belongs to God. So we must be very careful how we use money.

Again through Malachi, God reminded the people that a great day is coming when the Lord will rule. He promised that those who honor Him will see His power in their lives. "'But to you who fear My name/ The Sun of Righteousness shall arise/With healing in His wings . . .'" (Malachi 4:2).

God also made another wonderful promise. He promised to send messengers who "will turn the hearts of the fathers to the children,/And the hearts of the children to their fathers" (Malachi 4:6). When our hearts are turned to each other in love, then our families are happy. And that's what God wants.

Malachi's Example Teaches Us:
(1) We are to keep our family vows (see Malachi 2:14–16);

(2) We are to give God the money that belongs to Him (see Malachi 3:8–10).

Let's Pray Together:

In your own words, pray for each person in your family. Then, let's renew a promise to each other: "I love you! I will be loyal to you in this family for the rest of my life."

John the Baptist Pointing People to Jesus

Let's Remember:

". . . John saw Jesus coming toward him, and said, 'Behold! The Lamb of God who takes away the sin of the world!'" (John 1:29).

Let's Listen:

John the Baptist was the last great prophet before Jesus. God had called him to go into the wilderness to seek Him. Many people came to hear John preach about the Lord Jesus, who was soon to come. John cried, "'Prepare the way of the Lord,/Make His paths straight'" (Matthew 3:3). When the people confessed their sins, John baptized them in water. That is why he is called John the Baptist.

One day as John was baptizing, he saw the Lord Jesus coming toward him. He stopped and pointed the people to Jesus. John said, "Behold! The Lamb of God who takes away the sin of the world!" (John 1:29). Jesus asked John to baptize Him. John said, "I have need to be baptized by You, and are You coming to me?" Then Jesus said, "Permit it to be so now, for thus it is fitting for us to fulfill all righteousness" (Matthew 3:14–15).

Even though John was a popular preacher, he wanted the people to look to Jesus instead of him. John said of Jesus, "He must increase, but I must decrease" (John 3:30). Is that the way you feel? Do you want to point people to Jesus instead of yourself?

John was willing to get out of the spotlight so people could see Jesus. He told the people to look to the Lord Jesus because He alone could take away sin.

Jesus honored John for his humble heart. He said, "Assuredly, I say to you, among those born of women there has not risen one greater than John the Baptist . . ." (Matthew 11:11).

John the Baptist's Example Teaches Us:

(1) We should be willing to "take a back seat" to others (see John 3:30);

(2) We should always point people away from ourselves and to the Lord Jesus (see John 1:29).

Let's Pray Together:

Lord Jesus, may my life and my words always point others to You. In Your name, amen.

III.

Men and Women Who Changed The World

Adam and Eve In the Image of God

Let's Remember:

"So God created man in His own image; in the image of God He created him; male and female He created them" (Genesis 1:27).

Let's Listen:

How very much God loves people everywhere. God made you and He made you very special. You are very valuable to God.

You are not like the animals God made. People are the highest order God created. You were made to think, to love, and to make beautiful things, just like the One who created you. This is part of what it means to be made in the "image of God." And because we are made in God's own image, we are to behave ourselves and respect other people everywhere.

The first person God created was Adam. God placed him in a perfect garden called Eden.

> And the LORD God formed man of the dust of the ground, and breathed into his nostrils the breath of life; and man became a living being.
> The LORD God planted a garden eastward in Eden, and there He put the man whom He had formed (Genesis 2:7–8).

God knew that people are happiest together, rather than alone. So He made a wife for lonely Adam. "And the LORD God said, 'It is not good that man should be alone; I will make him a helper comparable to him'" (Genesis 2:18). God made the first woman, Eve, so she and Adam could enjoy life together, and so they could walk together with God.

God took a rib from the side of Adam and formed Eve after He had caused Adam to go into a deep sleep.

> And the LORD God caused a deep sleep to fall on Adam, and he slept; and He took one of his ribs, and closed up the flesh in its place. Then the rib which the LORD God had taken from man He made into a woman, and He brought her to the man. And Adam said:

"This is now bone of my bones
And flesh of my flesh;
She shall be called Woman,
Because she was taken out of Man" (Genesis 2:21–23).

Adam and Eve enjoyed walking with God in the garden. But one day they disobeyed God and sinned. Sin is going against what God says. God had told Adam and Eve not to eat of the tree of the knowledge of good and evil. But they disobeyed God and ate of the fruit of the tree.

Because of their sin, Adam and Eve no longer wanted to walk with God. Instead they tried to hide from Him. Isn't it like that with us too? When we do things that are wrong, we often want to hide from God.

But God still loved Adam and Eve. Although He was angry at their sin, He still wanted to forgive them so they could again walk and talk together. When we are walking with God and all of our sins are out of the way, the Bible calls this having fellowship with God (see 1 John 1:6–9). God called to Adam and said, "Where are you?" (Genesis 3:9). You see, God loves us enough to go searching for us, even when we disobey Him.

The devil, disguised as a serpent, had tempted Eve

and caused her to sin. God knew that all people would need someone to pay for their sins and destroy the devil's power. God promised Adam and Eve that one day His Son would come, born of a woman, to destroy the devil's power. "And I will put enmity/Between you and the woman," God told the devil, "And between your seed and her Seed;/He shall bruise your head,/And you shall bruise His heel" (Genesis 3:15).

God was telling the devil that one day Jesus would come. Even though the devil would try to destroy Him, Jesus would crush the devil's power. Isn't it wonderful? Even after Adam and Eve's sin, God promised to provide for their sin to be paid for. God loves us and He wants us to walk with Him.

Adam and Eve's Example Teaches Us:
(1) We are made in the image of God so we should respect ourselves and others (see Genesis 1:27);

(2) Sin breaks our fellowship with God. But when we come to Him He forgives us (see Genesis 3:15).

Let's Pray Together:
Thank You, God, that I am made in Your own image. Help me to respect myself and others. In Jesus' name, amen.

Cain and Abel
Your Brother's Keeper

Let's Remember:

"And the Lord respected Abel and his offering, but He did not respect Cain and his offering" (Genesis 4:4–5).

Let's Listen:

Adam and Eve had two sons. Their first son was named Cain. Their second son was named Abel. As these two boys grew older they came to worship the Lord and to bring a sacrifice to Him.

Abel brought an innocent animal and sacrificed it to the Lord. God approved this sacrifice because it helped the people understand that one day Jesus, the Lamb of God, would be sacrificed on the cross for the sins of the world.

Cain, on the other hand, brought God a sacrifice of

fruits and vegetables from his garden. He was giving God the best he could produce. But God wanted to show Cain that we are not accepted by Him because of what we can do. We are accepted by God because of Jesus' sacrifice for us. So the Bible says God respected Abel's sacrifice but He did not respect Cain's sacrifice. This means God accepted Abel's offering because Abel came to God in God's way.

You see, there are many sincere people who try to come to God in many different ways. But God only accepts those who come to Him in His way. Jesus said He is the only way to God. "I am the way, the truth and the life. No one comes to the Father except through Me" (John 14:6).

Cain was very angry because His offering had been rejected. He became jealous of his brother and angry at him. Because of this Cain did a horrible thing. He killed his brother, Abel. Do you see what terrible things can happen when we are jealous and angry?

After his terrible sin, Cain asked, "Am I my brother's keeper?" (Genesis 4:9). The answer is yes! We are responsible to take care of our brothers and sisters and not be angry at them or jealous of them.

Cain's and Abel's Examples Teach Us:
This story gives us a good example and a bad example.

(1) Abel's example teaches us that we must come to God in His way.

(2) Cain's bad example teaches us that we should never be angry at or jealous of our brothers or sisters. Instead, we should always look for ways to help and protect them.

Let's Pray Together:

Dear God, I always want to come to You in Your way. Keep me from being angry or jealous of others, even others in my family. In Jesus' name, amen.

Abraham
The Man of Faith

Let's Remember:

"'Abraham believed God, and it was accounted to him for righteousness'" (Romans 4:3).

Let's Listen:

One time God told Abraham just to get up and move, although He didn't tell him where. Abraham obeyed. Another time God promised Abraham a son even though he and his wife, Sarah, were very old. Again Abraham had faith in God. Then after his promised son, Isaac, was born, God tested Abraham's faith in a very big way. He told Abraham to sacrifice his son. Again Abraham was willing to obey. God stopped Abraham from sacrificing Isaac, but He saw that Abraham trusted God no matter what. Abraham fully trusted in what God promised.

Because Abraham had faith in God, God gave him wonderful promises. "I will bless those who bless you," God told Abraham, "And I will curse him who curses you; And in you all the families of the earth shall be blessed" (Genesis 12:3).

Abraham walked with God. One day the Lord came to Abraham in a vision and said, "Do not be afraid, Abram. I am your shield, your exceedingly great reward" (Genesis 15:1). Abraham's reward for obeying God was the presence of God Himself. In fact, God called Abraham His friend (see Isaiah 41:8). How wonderful it must have been for Abraham to be called a friend of God! You also can be a friend of God. If you obey Him, as Abraham did, you too can be a friend of God.

Many wonderful things happened to Abraham. Because he knew God so well, he was able to ask God boldly to spare an entire city from being destroyed. Yes, Abraham prayed for others.

Did you know your family is blessed today because of Abraham? Abraham's faith was rewarded in the birth of his son, Isaac. Through Abraham and Isaac's descendants, Jesus came into the world. Because of Jesus, the whole world, including your family, is blessed.

When we have faith in God as Abraham did, in God's eyes we become "children of Abraham" (see Galatians 3:7).

Abraham's Example Teaches Us:

(1) We should have faith in what God says (see Romans 4:3);

(2) We, too, can be friends of God (see Isaiah 41:8);

(3) We should pray for others (see Genesis 18:22–33).

Let's Pray Together:

Dear God, I want to be Your friend. Help me always to believe and obey what You say. In Jesus' name, amen.

Sarah
The Mother of Israel

Let's Remember:

"By faith Sarah herself also received strength to conceive seed, and she bore a child when she was past the age, because she judged Him faithful who had promised" (Hebrews 11:11).

Let's Listen:

Sarah was the beautiful wife of Abraham. God had made a promise to them that they would have a son. But years passed and they were still without a child. In fact, both Abraham and Sarah were about one hundred years old. Have you ever heard of anyone having children when they are one hundred years old?

It was past the time of life when women usually bear children. Yet Sarah hung on to the promise of God. Even though both Abraham and Sarah some-

times made mistakes, God stayed true to His promise. Isaac, the promised son, was born in due time.

Our verse says that God gave Sarah special strength to become a mother even when she was very old. This teaches us that when we place our faith in God, He will give us strength to serve Him and do His will both while we are young and when we grow old.

Sarah's Example Teaches Us:
God will give us strength to do His will when we trust Him.

Let's Pray Together:
Dear God, give me the gift of great faith in what You can do. In Jesus' name, amen.

Deborah
Courage Brings Victory

Let's Remember:
"'Hear, O kings! Give ear, O princes!/I, even I, will sing to the LORD;/I will sing praise to the LORD God of Israel'" (Judges 5:3).

Let's Listen:

Some people have worked for a long time to have a woman judge in the United States Supreme Court. But did you know that Israel had a woman judge thousands of years ago? Her name was Deborah.

God had called Deborah to be a leader of the people and a judge in Israel. This meant that her job was to encourage the people to live by God's law.

God had told Israel that He would give them victory over the enemy armies of Jabin. But Barak, the leader of Israel's armies, was afraid to obey and go into battle. "Hasn't the Lord promised us victory?" Deborah asked Barak. She urged Barak to obey the Lord's command.

Still Barak was afraid. "I'll go if you will go with me," Barak said finally.

"I will surely go with you; nevertheless there will be no glory for you in the journey you are taking, for the Lord will sell Sisera [the enemy] into the hand of a woman" (Judges 4:9).

The armies of Israel won the battle. They were led in triumph by this courageous woman, Deborah. After the battle, Deborah led the people in a victory song of praise to God. She reminded the people, "When leaders lead in Israel, when the people willingly offer themselves to the Lord, that is reason to bless the Lord" (see Judges 5:2).

God may ask you to do something that will demand that you be very brave. Others may be afraid to do the task God wants you to do. Take courage from Deborah. The Lord will use you to bring victory for His people. And when He does, like Deborah, give the Lord the glory.

Deborah's Example Teaches Us:

(1) When others are afraid, we should be brave in what God tells us to do;

(2) When God gives us victory, we must remember to praise Him.

Let's Pray Together:

Dear God, help me to be brave and do what You tell me to do. In Jesus' name, amen.

Hannah
A Mother Gives
Her Son to God

Let's Remember:

"'My heart rejoices in the LORD;/My [strength] is exalted in the LORD./I smile at my enemies,/Because I rejoice in Your salvation'" (1 Samuel 2:1).

Let's Listen:

One day Hannah was praying to God in the temple. Although she was loved very much by her husband, on that day she was very, very sad. For years she had wanted a son. But she and her husband Elkanah were still without children.

So Hannah cried out to God and said, "O LORD of hosts, if You will indeed look on the affliction of your maidservant and remember me, and . . . will give your maidservant a male child, then I will give him to the LORD all the days of his life . . ." (1 Samuel 1:11).

God heard Hannah's cry. Soon she gave birth to the child Samuel. Hannah kept her promise to God and gave him to the prophet Eli to raise in the house of the Lord. The Bible calls a promise we make to the Lord a vow. The Bible warns us, "When you make a vow to God, do not delay to pay it;/For He has no pleasure in fools./Pay what you have vowed./It is better not to vow than to vow and not pay" (Ecclesiastes 5:4). Hannah remembered to pay her vow.

Hannah was so happy when she became the mother of a son! Hannah knew what an honor it is to bear children and raise them for the Lord. She prayed to God again. This time it was not a prayer of sadness, but a song of joy. "My heart rejoices in the Lord," she sang. This prayer of thanksgiving became a favorite song of women in Israel.

Hundreds of years later, another woman found out she was going to have a baby. That woman was Mary. The angel had just announced to her that she would have the privilege of bringing God's Son, the Lord Jesus Christ, into the world.

When Mary heard this, she began to sing Hannah's song of praise to God. She sang out,

"My soul magnifies the Lord,
And my spirit has rejoiced in God my Savior.

For He has regarded the lowly state
   of His maidservant; . . .
For He who is mighty has done great things for me,
And Holy is His name" (Luke 1:46–49).

Mary was singing Hannah's song!

Hannah's Example Teaches Us:

(1) We must keep our promises to God (see Ecclesiastes 5:4);

(2) God can turn our sorrow into singing.

Let's Pray Together:

Thank You, God, that You answer prayer. Help me to always keep the promises I make to You. In Jesus' name, amen.

The Shunammite Woman A Notable Woman

Let's Remember:

"Now it happened one day that Elisha went to Shunem, where there was a notable woman . . ." (2 Kings 4:8).

Let's Listen:

We do not know the name of the woman of Shunem. But we do know the Bible calls her "a notable woman." This means she was a woman with whom God was pleased.

God's prophet Elisha often passed by the town of Shunem where this woman and her husband lived. She wanted to do something for God's prophet, so she and her husband built Elisha a room where he could rest.

In return for this kindness, Elisha asked the Shunammite woman what she wanted. He offered to put in a good word for her to the king. She said she was happy to live among her own people.

There was something, however, that this Shunammite woman wanted deeply. She wanted a son. Elisha foretold that she would indeed bear a son. In a year's time, this couple who had helped Elisha were the proud parents of a baby boy.

The baby grew into a fine little boy. One day as he was in the field with his father he suddenly yelled, "My head, my head!" (2 Kings 4:19). They carried the boy back home. His mother cared for him all morning but at noon the little boy died.

The broken-hearted mother took the little boy's body and laid it on the bed in Elisha's room. Then she ran to Elisha. Can you imagine how she must have felt as she was going to tell Elisha?

When she came near Elisha's dwelling, the prophet's servant asked this woman, "'Is it well with you? Is it well with your husband? Is it well with the child?' And she answered, 'It is well'" (2 Kings 4:26).

Elisha rushed back to the house with the mother when he heard what had happened. When Elisha went into the room where the young child's body lay, he believed God would perform a miracle. Life came back into the boy.

The Shunammite woman was overcome with joy. God had given back her son. Even after her son had died she could say, "Everything is all right." She was a notable woman because she had great faith in a God who can perform miracles.

The Shunammite Woman's Example Teaches Us:

Though your name, like that of this woman, may not go down in history, by your faith and obedience you can be forever noted by the Lord.

Let's Pray Together:

Help me, Lord, to live in such a way as to be noted by You. In Jesus' name, amen.

Mordecai
Loyalty in Crisis

Let's Remember:

"For Mordecai the Jew . . . was great among the Jews and well-received by the multitude of his brethren, seeking the good of his people and speaking peace to all his kindred" (Esther 10:3).

Let's Listen:

Mordecai was a Jew who lived away from his native land. He served King Ahasuerus, who ruled over a great kingdom all the way from India to Ethiopia. Even though Ahasuerus was not a Jew, Mordecai was loyal to him. This means he wanted only what was best for the king, and he never spoke against him. Many people were jealous of Mordecai because he was such a good friend of the king.

There came a time when Mordecai heard that two

enemies of King Ahasuerus were plotting to kill the ruler. Mordecai warned the king, and the king's life was spared. The evil men were punished with death (see Esther 2:21–23).

Another time, a wicked man named Haman tried to have Mordecai killed. Haman wanted Mordecai's place of honor with the king. Even though the king had honored Haman, Haman could not stand to see Mordecai honored too. The Bible tells the dramatic story of how Haman plotted to kill Mordecai in chapters 6 and 7 of the book of Esther. Haman even built gallows where he hoped to hang Mordecai. Instead, Haman himself was hanged, and Mordecai was brought to honor before the king.

It is important to know that Mordecai never sought to be honored or recognized. He simply was loyal to the king. Haman, on the other hand, was proud and boastful. He wanted to be exalted. Instead, he was brought down. Time after time the Bible warns us against pride. "'God resists the proud,/But gives grace to the humble'" (James 4:6).

Mordecai was the uncle of the king's wife, Esther. We will read about Esther later. God used Mordecai to give wise counsel to Queen Esther. In her hour of greatest testing, Mordecai urged her to be bold and stand up for God and His people. Mordecai was God's man in an important place.

Will you be loyal and stand for the Lord, just as Mordecai did?

Mordecai's Example Teaches Us:

(1) We are to always want the best for those who are over us;

(2) When we humble ourselves God will exalt us.

Let's Pray Together:

Dear God, make me a humble and loyal person. Then I know You will exalt me in Your own way and in Your time. In Jesus' name, amen.

Esther
For Such a Time as This

Let's Remember:

"'Yet who knows whether you have come to the kingdom for such a time as this?'" (Esther 4:14).

Let's Listen:

Esther was the beautiful queen of a great empire.

She was married to the mighty king Ahasuerus. But there was one problem in Esther's happy world as the queen. Some people hated all Jews and wanted to kill them. And Esther was a Jew.

The wicked man, Haman, had trapped the king into signing a decree "to destroy, to kill, and to annihilate all the Jews, both young and old, little children and women, in one day . . ." (Esther 3:13). The king did not know that his own wife was a Jew. Without knowing it, the king had signed a decree that meant his own wife would soon be killed!

We have already read of Esther's godly uncle, Mordecai. Mordecai told Esther that she need not think she would escape because she was the queen. "Who knows," Mordecai said to Esther, "you may have come to the kingdom for such a time as this" (Esther 4:14).

Esther knew she had a very big decision to make. She could try to hide from the problem. Or she could appeal to the king to save her people, the Jews. If she did this, her own life might be lost.

Esther decided to stand boldly. She told her uncle, "Go, gather all the Jews who are present in Shushan, and fast for me; neither eat nor drink for three days, night or day. My maids and I will fast likewise. And so I will go to the king, which is against the law; and if I perish, I perish!" (Esther 4:16).

The king granted Queen Esther's appeal to save the Jews. God used Esther to spare an entire race of people. She had chosen greatness.

Mordecai reminded Esther that God would deliver His people. If Esther was not willing to be His tool, God would raise up someone else. "But you, Esther, have a chance for greatness," Mordecai reminded her.

One day you may have a chance for greatness too. Along with Esther, you and I need to be willing to risk our lives for what is right.

Esther's Example Teaches Us:

(1) We should always defend God's people;

(2) We should be willing to lay down our lives for others.

Let's Pray Together:

Dear God, help me to be willing even to risk my life in standing for what is right. In Jesus' name, amen.

Nehemiah
Rebuilding the Walls

Let's Remember:
"'The God of heaven Himself will prosper us; therefore we His servants will arise and build . . .'" (Nehemiah 2:20).

Let's Listen:
Nehemiah, like Mordecai, worked for a king.

Nehemiah was the cupbearer for the great King Artaxerxes. But Nehemiah was sad when he thought of his hometown, Jerusalem. The city was torn down. No longer was it a strong, beautiful city. Now it lay in ruins.

But God put a vision in Nehemiah's heart to rebuild the walls of Jerusalem and make the city beautiful again. He asked permission from the king to leave and go back to Jerusalem to do this important work.

The king granted his request and Nehemiah left for Jerusalem with hope in his heart.

When he told the people of Jerusalem his dream of a restored city, they took courage and decided to help Nehemiah. The people became so excited they said, "'Let us rise up and build.' Then they set their hands to do this good work" (Nehemiah 2:18).

But not everyone liked Nehemiah's idea. Many people questioned him and tried to anger him. They teased Nehemiah and told him it couldn't be done. Nehemiah answered them, "The God of heaven Himself will prosper us; therefore we His servants will arise and build . . ." (Nehemiah 2:20).

In the middle of this important project, some people tried to get Nehemiah in a debate about whether or not the walls should be rebuilt and why. But Nehemiah would not turn away from his task. "I am doing a great work, so that I cannot come down," he replied. "Why should the work cease while I leave it and go down to you?" (Nehemiah 6:3).

Nehemiah stayed right with the job and in just a short time the walls of Jerusalem were rebuilt. The city was strong once again.

God wants you to be a rebuilder too. He may not ask you to rebuild walls. God may want you to rebuild lives that have been torn down. We should all be building up other people. When it comes to how we treat other people,

> A good thing to remember
> And a better thing to do
> Is to work with the construction gang
> Not with the wrecking crew!

Nehemiah's Example Teaches Us:
(1) We should attempt to do what God puts in our hearts;

(2) We should not become discouraged when people try to keep us from our task.

Let's Pray Together:
Dear God, give me strength to finish the things that You put in my heart to do. In Jesus' name, amen.

Mary
A Very Special
Assignment

Let's Remember:

"Then Mary said, 'Behold the maidservant of the Lord! Let it be to me according to your word'" (Luke 1:38).

Let's Listen:

Mary was a young Jewish girl with a happy future. She was engaged to be married to Joseph.

One day something amazing happened to her. An angel of the Lord appeared to Mary. "Rejoice, highly favored one, the Lord is with you; blessed are you among women!" the angel said (Luke 1:28). The angel told her, ". . . you have found favor with God. And behold, you will conceive in your womb and bring forth a Son, and shall call His name JESUS" (Luke 1:30–31).

The angel went on to explain that the Holy Spirit would overshadow Mary, and that the Holy One born of her would be the Son of God.

God was changing Mary's plans for her future. But Mary was willing to obey. She said, "Let it be to me according to your word" (Luke 1:38).

God the Father chose Mary for the wonderful assignment of bringing God the Son, Jesus Christ, into the world through God the Holy Spirit. One reason Mary became the most blessed among women was because she lived a pure life. Another reason God chose Mary is because she had hidden His Word in her heart. When Mary knew God was using her to bring Jesus into the world, she thanked God for this blessing by prayers out of the Bible. She sang Hannah's song, "'My soul magnifies the Lord,/And my spirit has rejoiced in God my Savior'" (Luke 1:47).

Mary's Example Teaches Us:

(1) We should be willing to obey what God wants us to do;

(2) We should live pure lives before the Lord;

(3) We should memorize God's Word.

Let's Pray Together:

Dear God, I know You have an assignment for me, too. Help me to be willing to do whatever You ask of me. In Jesus' name, amen.

Philip
The First Evangelist

Let's Remember:

"Then Philip went down to the city of Samaria and preached Christ to them" (Acts 8:5).

Let's Listen:

Do you know what an evangelist is? An evangelist is someone who tells other people about Jesus. When we think of an evangelist we usually think of someone like Billy Graham. But do you know who the first Christian evangelist was? The first evangelist was Philip.

Philip had faithfully served the Lord as a helper in the church in Jerusalem. Evil people who were angry at the new Christians drove them out of their homes and away from their families. When Philip had to leave Jerusalem he journeyed north into Samaria, preaching in all the cities the good news of Jesus.

Under Philip's preaching, many people gave their lives to Jesus and became part of the church. God did wonderful things for them. Sick people were made well, and people who had been tormented by the devil were freed by the power of God. This made everyone in Samaria very happy. The Bible says, "There was great joy in that city" (Acts 8:8).

In the middle of this large meeting God had another job for His evangelist. An angel of the Lord spoke to Philip and told him to go into the desert. Philip immediately obeyed. In the desert he met an important man from Ethiopia who was seeking to know God.

Philip was still doing his job as an evangelist. But now he was not preaching to great crowds. Now he was talking with one person about his need for Jesus. The man from Ethiopia believed in Jesus when Philip shared the good news with him.

After Philip had baptized his new Christian friend, an amazing thing happened. The Bible says that the Spirit of the Lord caught Philip away so that the man did not see him any more! (See Acts 8:39.)

You may never be an evangelist who preaches to huge crowds of people. But in one way, all Christians should be evangelists. We should all tell others about Jesus.

Philip's Example Teaches Us:

(1) If we serve God in the small things, He will honor us with greater things (see Acts 8:4–5);

(2) We should be ready to tell others about Jesus (see 1 Peter 3:15);

(3) In God's eyes, one person is as important as a large crowd of people (see Acts 8:26).

Let's Pray Together:

Lord Jesus, make me excited about telling others of Your love for them. In Your name, amen.

Paul the Apostle A Changed Life

Let's Remember:

"Therefore, if anyone is in Christ, he is a new creation; old things have passed away; behold, all things have become new" (2 Corinthians 5:17).

Let's Listen:

Saul was a leader of his people. He was one of the most educated people of his day. He had been trained to hate the followers of Jesus and all they stood for.

Saul had made it his business to try to stamp out the new Christian faith. One day he was making a trip to the city of Damascus to put Christians in prison. As he was on the road a bright light shone out of heaven. The Lord Himself appeared to Saul and said, "Saul, Saul, why are you persecuting Me?" (Acts 9:4).

Saul was very frightened and asked, "Who are You, Lord?" (Acts 9:5).

The Lord said, "I am Jesus, whom you are persecuting" (Acts 9:5).

On that day Saul became a follower of Jesus. New Christian friends like Barnabas helped introduce Saul to his new brothers and sisters in Christ. Saul became a brand-new person. He even received a new name. Instead of being called Saul, now he was called Paul.

Paul went everywhere telling people about Jesus. Many people were not happy that Paul had a new life. Often Paul was beaten, yelled at, and hated because of his love for Jesus. Still Paul stayed true to the Lord Jesus, his dearest Friend. Paul said his desire was "that I may know Him and the power of His resurrection, and the fellowship of His sufferings, being conformed to His death" (Philippians 3:10).

Paul wanted the whole world to hear the message of Jesus. He made several missionary trips to tell people the good news. Now Christians understood that the good news of Jesus was not just for one nation, but for the entire world. Because Paul took the message of Jesus into other lands, you and I have the message of Jesus today.

Although he had many enemies, Paul also had many friends. He helped young preachers like Timothy learn how to serve the Lord well. God gave Paul a long, happy life serving Him.

Paul was proud of the Lord Jesus and the message about Him. He said, "I am not ashamed of the gospel of Christ, for it is the power of God to salvation for everyone who believes . . ." (Romans 1:16).

Paul's Example Teaches Us:

(1) When we come to Jesus He gives us a new life (see 2 Corinthians 5:17);

(2) We should want Jesus to be our dearest Friend (see Philippians 3:10);

(3) We should be proud of Jesus and the message about Him (see Romans 1:16).

Let's Pray Together:

Thank You, Lord Jesus, for giving me a new life. Help me tell others the good news that You want to give them a new life too. In Your name, amen.

Lydia Thankful for Salvation

Let's Remember:

"And when [Lydia] and her household were baptized, she begged us, saying, 'If you have judged me to be faithful to the Lord, come to my house and stay'" (Acts 16:15).

Let's Listen:

Do you know who the first Christian in Europe was? The first Christian in Europe was a lady named Lydia. Here is the story of how she came to Jesus.

"Now a certain woman named Lydia heard us [Paul and his missionary companions]. She was a seller of purple from the city of Thyatira, who worshiped God. The Lord opened her heart to heed the things spoken by Paul. And when she and her household were baptized, she begged us, saying, 'If you have judged me to be faithful to the Lord, come to my house and stay.' And she constrained us" (Acts 16:14–15).

Lydia sold purple dye for a living. Her heart was hungry to know God. When Paul came to her city and preached the good news of Jesus, she opened her heart.

Lydia was so thankful that she belonged to Jesus. She wanted to do something to show the Lord how grateful she was to Him. So she urged Paul and his friends to stay at her house. No doubt she cooked wonderful meals for the missionaries.

Lydia became a friend of the apostle Paul and his companions. They would later come back to Lydia's house again. They had found someone who was thankful for her salvation.

Lydia's Example Teaches Us:

We should show our thanks to God for salvation by helping those who preach the gospel.

Let's Pray Together:

Dear God, thank You for all Your blessings to me. Most of all, thank You for the Lord Jesus. In His name, amen.

IV.

The Followers of Jesus

Andrew
He Brought His
Brother to Jesus

Let's Remember:

"[Andrew] first found his own brother Simon, and said to him, 'We have found the Messiah' (which is translated, the Christ). And he brought him to Jesus" (John 1:41–42).

Let's Listen:

Andrew was a disciple of John the Baptist who came to follow Jesus. Andrew was convinced that Jesus was the true One sent from God. He was so glad finally to meet God's Son.

After Andrew met Jesus, the first thing he did was to go and tell his brother Simon. Andrew was excited. He exclaimed to his brother, "We have found Him! Now we know who the Messiah is!" Then he brought his brother to Jesus. When Simon met Jesus he, too, was sure Jesus was the Son of God.

We don't know much else about Andrew's life. But we hear a lot about his brother, Simon Peter. Peter became much more famous than Andrew. But what an important job Andrew did! It was Andrew who brought Simon Peter to Jesus.

Have you ever thought of this? You may never become famous. But you may introduce someone else to Jesus who will do great things for God. Then you will have a part in their reward.

History tells us that Andrew died by being hung on a cross, just like his Lord. The story of Andrew's love for Jesus spread to many parts of the world, including Scotland. There, missionaries told others about Jesus, just as Andrew had told his brother.

Andrew's Example Teaches Us:
When we meet Jesus we must tell others about Him.

Let's Pray Together:
Dear Lord Jesus, I'm so glad that I have met You. Now help me to introduce You to others. In Your name, amen.

James and John
The Sons of Thunder

Let's Remember:

"And going on from there, He saw two other brothers, James the son of Zebedee, and John his brother, in the boat with Zebedee their father, mending their nets. And He called them, and immediately they left the boat and their father, and followed Him" (Matthew 4:21–22).

Let's Listen:

It was quite a crew of young men who followed Jesus. Several of them had been tough, mean fishermen.

James and John were two brothers with angry tempers. But when they came to Jesus He began to change them.

From among the twelve disciples, Jesus picked

three to go with Him on very special occasions. The three He chose were Peter, James, and John. They went with Him when He raised a person from the dead, and when He was transfigured in heavenly glory.

Sometimes James and John let their anger get the best of them. Sometimes they were self-seeking. But with all their faults, they were ready at any time to give their lives for Jesus.

In fact, James became the first apostle to be killed for the cause of Jesus. Wicked King Herod was angry at the strong growth of the young church. To show his anger he killed James with a sword.

John, like his older brother James, was a fighter. Jesus nicknamed James and John the "Sons of Thunder" (see Mark 3:17) because they always seemed ready for action.

But Jesus changed these brothers completely. John became known in his later life not as a fighter but as the apostle of love. It was John who was closest to Jesus at the Last Supper. It was John who stayed with Jesus at His death when the other disciples had deserted Him. And while James was the first apostle to die, John was the last.

John wrote five books of the Bible. The great theme in his letters was, "Beloved, let us love one another, for love is of God; and everyone who loves is born of God and knows God" (1 John 4:7).

Do you sometimes get mad and want to fight? As He did for James and John, Jesus can give you a heart of love for Him and for others. He will use your energy for good.

James and John's Example Teaches Us:
(1) God can use us even with our faults;
(2) God can change us and take away our faults;
(3) God can use our energy for good.

Let's Pray Together:
Dear God, thank You for making me active. Take my energy and use it for good. In Jesus' name, amen.

Judas The Traitor

Let's Remember:
"'I have sinned by betraying innocent blood'" (Matthew 27:4).

144

Let's Listen:

Not much good can be said of Judas. He is put in this book because we need to learn from bad examples as well as good examples.

Judas was very greedy. He was the treasurer for Jesus and the disciples, but he often stole money for himself. Jesus lovingly rebuked Judas for his love of money. This made Judas so angry that he looked for a way to betray Jesus and turn Him over to His enemies.

Judas made a deal to sell Jesus to His enemies by putting them in a place where they could catch Him. The price they paid to Judas for betraying Jesus was thirty pieces of silver, the price paid for a slave.

After he betrayed Jesus, Judas felt the guilt of his awful sin. He died a terrible death by hanging himself.

Judas's big problem was that he let his love for money overrule his love for his friends.

Judas's Bad Example Teaches Us:

(1) We should not be greedy for money;

(2) We should never let our love for things make us disloyal to our friends.

Let's Pray Together:

Dear God, keep me free from greed. Help me always to be loyal to my friends and especially to You. In Jesus' name, amen.

Matthew
A Party for Jesus

Let's Remember:

"Then as Jesus passed on from there, He saw a man named Matthew sitting at the tax office. And He said to him, 'Follow Me.' And he arose and followed Him" (Matthew 9:9).

Let's Listen:

Matthew was a tax collector. He worked for the government of Rome. Because of this, he was hated by many of his fellow Jews. But Jesus loved Matthew and wanted him to find happiness.

One day Jesus passed by Matthew's office. He simply said, "Follow Me." At that command, Matthew left his good job to become a follower of Jesus.

Matthew was so happy that he had found new life in

Jesus. He wanted all his friends to know Jesus too. So, do you know what he did? He had a big dinner party to introduce all his friends to Jesus.

He called all the other tax collectors in town. Other people came to the party who were thought of as "sinners" by the religious people. Jesus was glad to come to the party and eat a meal with these people who so badly needed Him.

The religious people asked, "Why is Jesus eating with such bad people?" (see Luke 5:30).

Jesus answered them, "Those who are well do not need a physician, but those who are sick. I have not come to call the righteous, but sinners, to repentance" (Luke 5:31–32).

When Matthew came to Jesus he wanted all his friends to meet Jesus, too.

Matthew's Example Teaches Us:

(1) Even if others don't like us, Jesus loves us;

(2) When we meet Jesus, we should want our friends to meet Him too.

Let's Pray Together:

Dear God, help me think of special ways to introduce my friends to Jesus. In His name, amen.

Mary Magdalene
A Life That Says
"Thank You"

Let's Remember:

"Mary Magdalene . . . also followed [Jesus] and ministered to Him . . ." (Mark 15:40–41).

Let's Listen:

Mary Magdalene had many reasons to be thankful. Before she met Jesus she lived a shameful life. She had even lost control of her actions and had been overtaken by evil spirits.

Then she met Jesus. He drove the evil spirits away from her and gave her a brand-new life. "If anyone is in Christ, he is a new creation; old things have passed away; behold, all things have become new" (2 Corinthians 5:17). Mary knew this was true because it happened to her.

From that wonderful day when she first met the

Lord, Mary began to look for ways she could say thank you to Jesus. The Bible says she "followed Him and ministered to Him" (Mark 15:41).

We know that Jesus ministers to us. But have you thought about how you can minister to Him? We minister to Jesus, or say thank you to Him, when we live for Him and try to please Him in all we do.

Mary's Example Teaches Us:

Our lives should be one big thank you to Jesus for giving us a new life in Him.

Let's Pray Together:

Dear Lord Jesus, may everything I do be my way of saying thanks to You for giving me a new life. In Your name, amen.

Simon Peter
A Bold Stand for Jesus

Let's Remember:

"For we did not follow cunningly devised fables when we made known to you the power and coming

of our Lord Jesus Christ, but were eyewitnesses of His majesty" (2 Peter 1:16).

Let's Listen:

Peter loved adventure! He was willing to try almost anything. When the other disciples were afraid, Peter walked on water to Jesus. He was ready to fight for Jesus, build temples for Jesus, or preach for Jesus. More than once Peter's brash attitude got him into trouble. But always Jesus loved him.

One day Jesus asked his disciples, "Who do you say that I am?" Peter was quick to answer, "You are the Christ, the Son of the living God" (Matthew 16:16).

Sometimes Peter was too quick to make promises. Just before Jesus was taken from His disciples, Peter said he would be willing to die for the Lord. But in just a few hours he denied Jesus three times. Can you imagine how Peter must have felt when Jesus looked at him after he had denied Him?

The Bible says Peter wept bitterly because he had denied the Lord (see Matthew 26:75).

But Peter was present at the empty tomb, and he saw Jesus after He rose from the dead. Peter knew he was not following just another man. He knew Jesus was the Christ, the Son of the living God.

Peter became one of the great leaders of the new Christian church. After he was filled with the Holy

Spirit on the day of Pentecost, he preached a sermon and three thousand people were added to the church.

God blessed Peter and gave him special power. Many people were healed by God's power when Peter prayed for them. He lived a happy life telling others about Jesus and wrote two books in the Bible. Yes, Peter took a bold stand for Jesus.

Peter's Example Teaches Us:

(1) We should watch what we say. Our words can get us in trouble;

(2) We should boldly take our stand for Jesus.

Let's Pray Together:

Lord Jesus, help me to take a bold stand for You wherever I am. In Your name, amen.

Thomas
Doubt Becomes Faith

Let's Remember:

"Thomas . . . said to Him, 'My Lord and my God!'" (John 20:28).

Let's Listen:

Often we have called this disciple "doubting Thomas."

Thomas was not present when Jesus appeared to the other disciples after He rose from the dead. Because of this, Thomas was not quick to believe that Jesus had indeed risen from the dead. He said, "Unless I see in His hands the print of the nails, and put my finger into the print of the nails, and put my hand in His side, I will not believe" (John 20:25).

Then Jesus appeared to Thomas, too. In a moment, all his doubt was gone. He worshiped his living Lord and exclaimed, "My Lord and my God!" (John 20:28). Saint Augustine said about Thomas, "He doubted that we might not doubt."

But Thomas was also a devoted follower of Jesus. When the other disciples were afraid to go into Judea, where some people had threatened to kill Jesus, Thomas urged them, "Let us also go, that we may die with Him" (John 11:16).

Once Jesus was talking to the disciples about the way to heaven and God the Father. Thomas asked, "Lord, how can we know the way?" Jesus answered, "I am the way, the truth, and the life. No one comes to the Father except through Me" (John 14:6).

After Thomas saw the risen Lord, he spent the rest

of his life telling people that the way to heaven is through coming to Christ. He traveled by foot and horseback all the way to India to tell people the good news of Jesus. There he was killed for his faith in the living Lord Jesus.

Thomas was no longer a doubter. His doubt was turned to solid faith.

Thomas's Example Teaches Us:

(1) We do not need to doubt any more. Jesus has shown Himself to be alive;

(2) We should be willing to die for Jesus.

Let's Pray Together:

Lord Jesus, right now I speak my faith. I know You are alive! Amen.

V.

Above All Others

Jesus
God's Eternal Son

Let's Remember:

"Jesus Christ is the same yesterday, today, and forever" (Hebrews 13:8).

Let's Listen:

Jesus is God's eternal Son. He is fully God and fully man.

Jesus came to earth to show us what God is like and to tell us how much He loves us.

Jesus lived a life without any sin. Then, one day, He died on the cross for us. His blood became the payment for all our sins. "For Christ also suffered once for sins, the just for the unjust, that He might bring us to God . . ." (1 Peter 3:18).

Have you turned from your sins and asked Jesus to come into your life? When you do that, God forgives

you of your sins. You become a brand new person. "Therefore, if anyone is in Christ, he is a new creation; old things have passed away; behold, all things have become new" (2 Corinthians 5:17).

Jesus is alive today. He rules over heaven and earth and lives inside those who come to Him. Our verse reminds us that Jesus is the same yesterday, today, and forever. He is doing today what He has always done. He is still taking broken, unhappy lives, placing them in His church and making them new people.

In this book we have been looking at the examples of many people. But there is one life and one example that is above all others. Peter said, "For to this you were called, because Christ also suffered for us, leaving us an example, that you should follow His steps" (1 Peter 2:21).

How wonderful that, since Jesus lives inside us, He gives us the power to follow Him and be like Him.

Jesus' Example Teaches Us:

Just as Jesus relied on His Father to do God's will, so we must rely on Jesus to do God's will.

Let's Pray Together:

If you have not turned from your sins and given your life to Jesus, let this prayer be yours:

"Lord Jesus, thank You for dying for me. I'm sorry for my sins. I turn away from them now, and I turn to You. I trust You and You alone to get to heaven. I take You now as my personal Savior. I will follow You as my Lord for the rest of my life. Thank You for hearing my prayer, forgiving my sins, and coming into my life. Amen."

If you have already given your life to Jesus, tell Him now how much you love Him in your own words.